STICKER BOOKS
OUTER SPACE

THE WONDERS OF SPACE

For thousands of years, people have been trying to unravel the mysteries of what lies beyond our planet Earth. Modern telescopes and spacecraft have told us much about the wonders of the Universe. They have also reminded us of how little we really know about space, and how much more there is to learn.

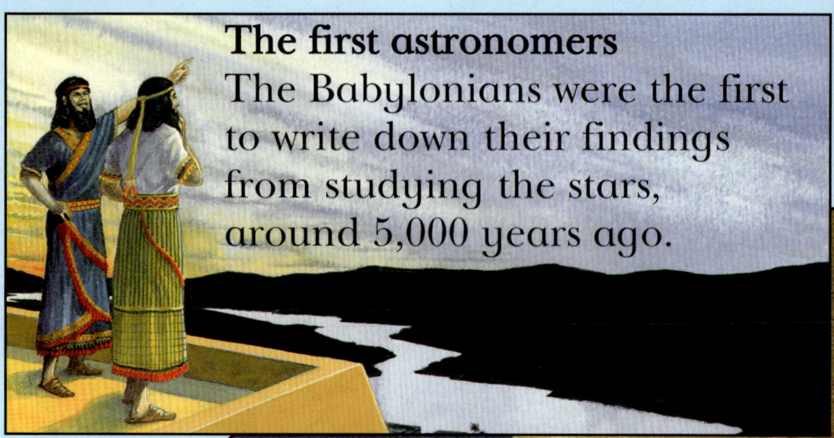

The first astronomers
The Babylonians were the first to write down their findings from studying the stars, around 5,000 years ago.

Where we are
People once thought Earth was at the center of the Universe. Now we know that our Solar System is one of billions in our galaxy. And our galaxy is just one of billions in a vast Universe!

Our Solar System

Local stars

Our galaxy
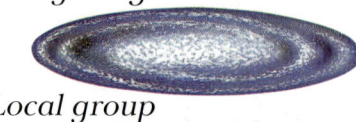

Local group of galaxies

Local super group of galaxies

The Universe

Probes
Perhaps, billions of years in the future, space probes from Earth will travel beyond our galaxy.

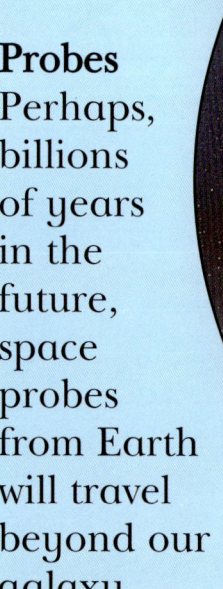

Our galaxy

The first rockets
The Chinese made the first "rockets" about 1,000 years ago, but they were more like fireworks than today's rockets. They were flaming arrows that were fired from a basket, using gunpowder.

An Ancient Chinese "rocket" being fired

Round, not flat

Aristotle realised that the Earth must be round in the 330s BC. He worked this out when he saw the circular shadow of the Earth on the Moon, during an eclipse.

The Ancient Greek thinker Aristotle

Stationary star

The only star that doesn't appear to move is above the North Pole. Sailors used the pole star to help them navigate – it's lowest at the Equator.

Path of the stars with the pole star in the middle

The first telescopes

The Italian astronomer Galileo was the first person to use a telescope to look at the night sky. He discovered four of Jupiter's moons.

Galileo Galilei

The modern American space shuttle

THE SOLAR SYSTEM

Our Solar System is centered around the Sun. It includes the family of nine planets orbiting (traveling around) the Sun, as well as the moons of these planets, and smaller objects, such as comets, asteroids and space rock.

The gas giants
Jupiter and Saturn are planets known as "gas giants." This is because they both have a small rocky center, surrounded by a surface made up of gas. We could never land spacecraft on the gas giants.

The inner planets
The four planets closest to the Sun are known as the inner planets. The "asteroid belt" – a cluster of lumps of space rock, orbiting the Sun – lies between Mars and Jupiter.

Saturn
Distance from Sun
885 million miles
Diameter
80,389 miles

Jupiter
Distance from Sun
482 million miles
Diameter
88,650 miles

Mercury
Distance from Sun
36 million miles
Diameter
3,024 miles

Venus
Distance from Sun
67 million miles
Diameter
7,504 miles

Earth
Distance from Sun
93 million miles
Diameter
7,909 miles

Mars
Distance from Sun
141 million miles
Diameter
4,214 km

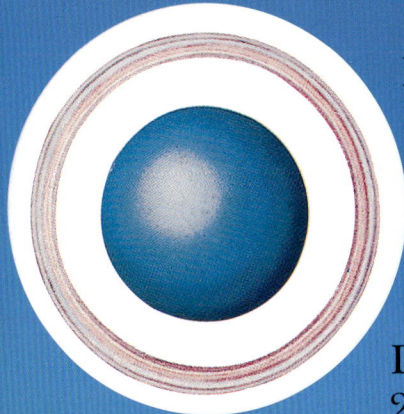

Uranus
Distance from Sun
1,179 million miles
Diameter
31,693 miles

Neptune
Distance from Sun
2,788 million miles
Diameter
30,710 miles

Pluto
Distance from Sun
3,658 million miles
Diameter
1,463 miles

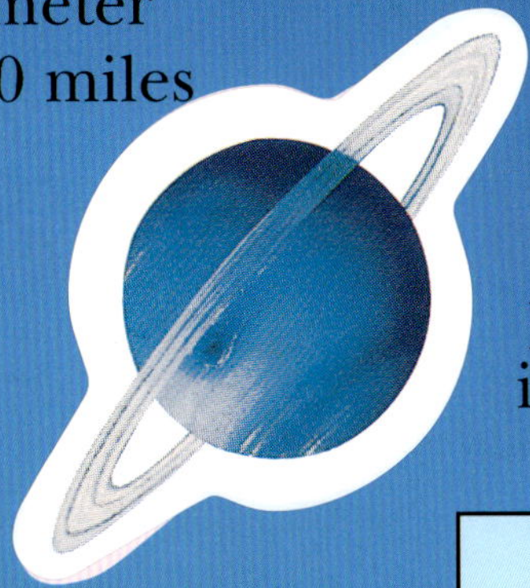

Our Moon
Most of the planets have natural satellites that orbit them. The Earth's satellite is the Moon. Because the Moon has no atmosphere to protect it, its rocky surface is constantly pelted by space rocks. These impacts cause craters.

The Moon

The outer planets
The three planets farthest from the Sun are freezing, hostile places. Conditions there are much too cold to sustain any sort of life.

The Sun
The closest star to the Earth is our Sun. It is a shining ball of gas which is over 25,000,000° at its center. Its gravity stops the planets from flying off into space.

The Sun

Moons
Jupiter has no fewer than 17 moons. Galileo discovered the four biggest in 1610 – Callisto, Ganymede, Europa and Io. Ganymede is the largest moon in the Solar System, and even bigger than the planet Mercury.

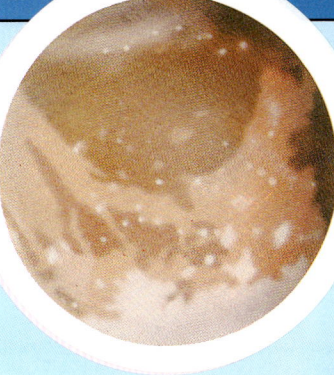

Ganymede

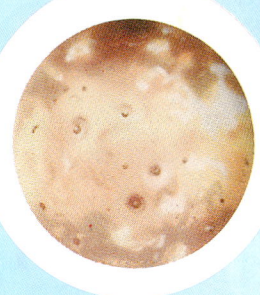

Io

Europa

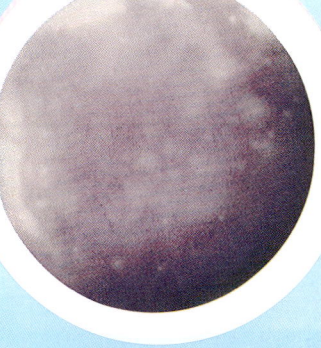

Callisto

5

MAN IN SPACE

Just 75 years ago, the idea of space travel was pure science fiction. People could only dream of flying beyond Earth's atmosphere or setting foot on other worlds. Yet today, space missions are being undertaken every day of the year.

The first astronaut
The first living thing to travel to space was a Russian dog called Laika, in late 1957.

First man in space
A young Russian pilot called Yuri Gagarin was the first person in space, in 1961. He orbited the Earth for two hours.

First woman in space
The first woman in space was also a Russian. Valentina Tereshkova made a three-day journey into space in 1963.

Man on the Moon
Although the first people in space were Russian, only American astronauts have ever landed on the Moon. There were six Moon landings in total, the last in 1972.

The space race
Wernher von Braun invented the deadly German V2 rocket missile during World War II. After the war, the Americans recruited von Braun to help them develop their new space program.

Americans in space
John Glenn was the first American to orbit the Earth, in a Mercury capsule.

Armstrong and Aldrin
Neil Armstrong was the first person to set foot on the Moon, in 1969, closely followed by Buzz Aldrin. They collected rocks to take home.

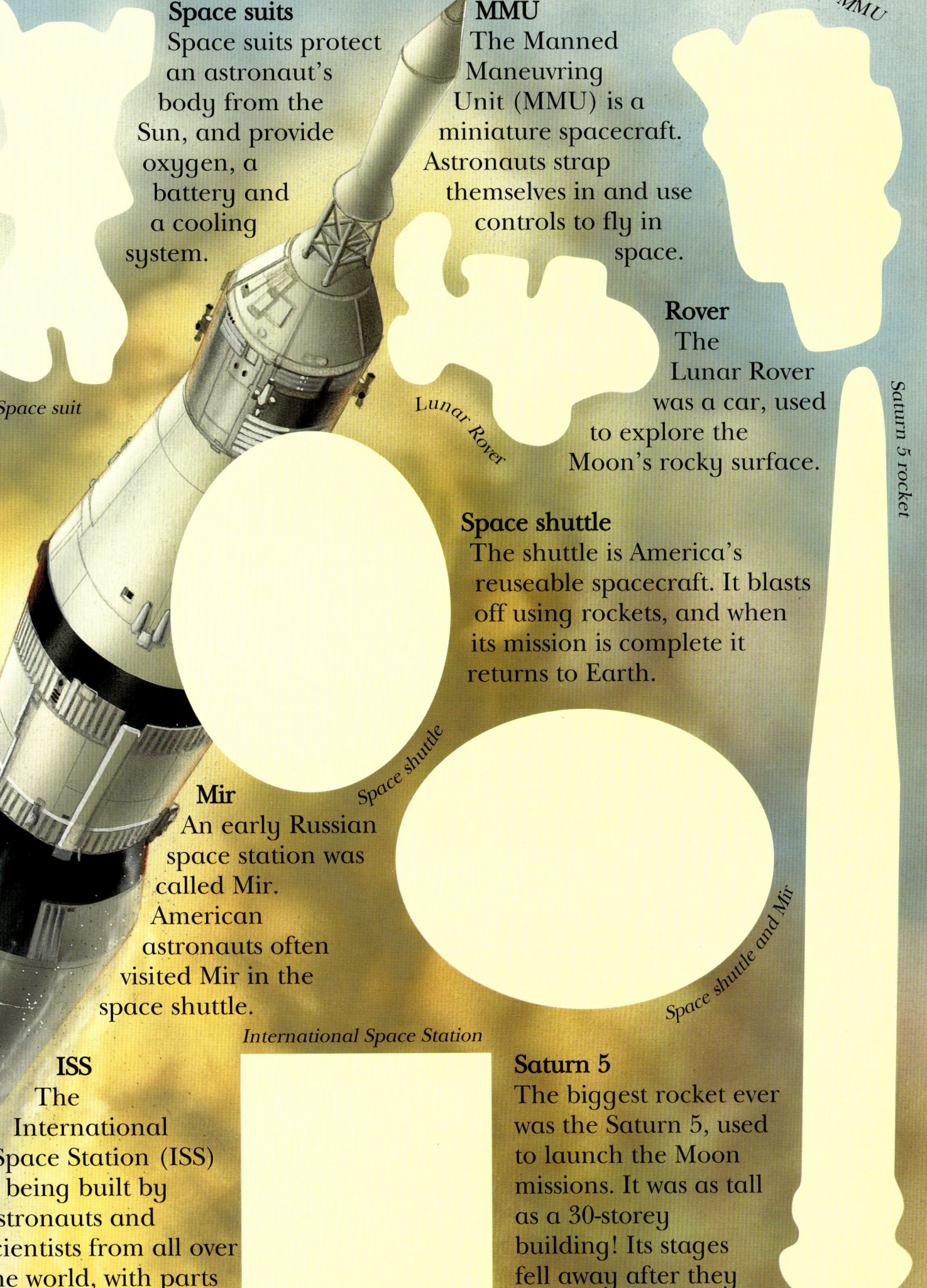

Space suits
Space suits protect an astronaut's body from the Sun, and provide oxygen, a battery and a cooling system.

Space suit

MMU
The Manned Maneuvring Unit (MMU) is a miniature spacecraft. Astronauts strap themselves in and use controls to fly in space.

MMU

Rover
The Lunar Rover was a car, used to explore the Moon's rocky surface.

Lunar Rover

Space shuttle
The shuttle is America's reuseable spacecraft. It blasts off using rockets, and when its mission is complete it returns to Earth.

Space shuttle

Saturn 5 rocket

Mir
An early Russian space station was called Mir. American astronauts often visited Mir in the space shuttle.

Space shuttle and Mir

ISS
The International Space Station (ISS) is being built by astronauts and scientists from all over the world, with parts delivered by shuttle.

International Space Station

Saturn 5
The biggest rocket ever was the Saturn 5, used to launch the Moon missions. It was as tall as a 30-storey building! Its stages fell away after they had done their job.

7

EXPLORING SPACE

Men have only traveled as far as the Moon. But unmanned spacecraft have traveled much farther, looking at the planets and even beyond.

Copernicus

Around the Sun
Nicolaus Copernicus first explained that the planets travel around the Sun, in 1543. Few people believed him.

Sputnik 1

First satellite
Sputnik 1 was the first man-made satellite to orbit the Earth, in 1957. It was tiny – less than 2 feet across!

Too hot to handle
At 900°, Venus is the hottest planet in the Solar System. Four unmanned Venera probes have landed there, but soon broke down in the heat.

Venera probe

Robot car
The Pathfinder probe landed on Mars in 1997. It carried the Sojourner robot car, which sent pictures of Mars back to Earth.

Telescopes
The best way of getting a good look at the night sky is with a telescope. The lenses and mirrors in telescopes make far-away objects seem much closer. The most sophisticated telescope is Hubble, which orbits the Earth, taking clear pictures of objects billions of miles away.

Early telescope

Hubble Space Telescope

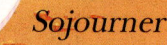
Sojourner

Triton
Neptune's moon Triton is one of the coldest places ever recorded. It only reaches minus 393°!

Surface of Triton

Galaxies
There are three basic galaxy shapes – spiral, oval or elliptical and irregular. Of course, irregular just means no particular shape! Each galaxy is unique.

Oval galaxy

Irregular galaxy

Spiral galaxy

Comets
Comets are often compared to huge, dusty snowballs racing through space.

White dwarves
A white dwarf is a dying star. Its gas has burnt off, and only a planet-sized, white-hot dense core remains.

White dwarf

Pulsars
Tiny, dense neutron stars (the remains of exploding stars) flash out light and radio signals as they rapidly spin. These incredible stars are called pulsars.

Pulsar

Red giants
A red giant is an old star that has swollen up. Depending on how big it gets, it might blow up or fade out.

Red giant

Dark matter
Scientists know that there is matter in the Universe that they can't see. They call this dark matter.

Dark matter

STICKER BOOKS
OCEANS

WATER WORLD

From the moment people began to populate Earth they have been inspired by the oceans. Some people have explored its depths with sophisticated submarines. Others have studied the extraordinary life forms that inhabit it. All kinds of manmade vessels have sailed or flown over its surface.

Viking longship

Surfer

Enjoying the waves
Surfers ride along the sloping faces of waves balanced on their boards. Expert surfers can stay on a wave all the way to the shore. They often ride through the "tube" formed by the curling crest of the wave.

Ancient mariners
About 1,000 years ago, Viking warriors sailed the oceans in their longships. These were sleek wooden ships with a single square sail, used for exploring and launching raids. When the wind blew from the wrong direction, or stopped blowing altogether, they would have to row instead.

Blue planet
It looks beautiful–blue with swirling white clouds. Astronauts in space spend most of their free time gazing at it. They can even make out cities, when they are lit up at night with twinkling lights. As far as we know, Earth is the only planet in the Solar System that has life. As well as warmth from the Sun, the other main requirement for life is liquid water. Earth has plenty of water–in total, it covers about three-quarters of the planet's surface!

Earth seen from space

Papyrus reed boat Ra II

Marine iguana

Living by the ocean
The marine iguana lives on the Galapagos Islands. It loves eating seaweed. At low tide, it dives into the water and clings on to a weed-covered rock with its claws. It tears off the seaweed with its mouth.

Sailing across the seas
In 1970, Thor Heyerdahl, a Norwegian scientist and explorer, and his seven crew, crossed the Atlantic Ocean in a sailing boat made from reeds. The trip showed that sailors from Ancient Egypt could have made the journey in reed boats thousands of years before Christopher Columbus in 1492.

Flying across the seas
In 1928, Australians Charles Kingsford Smith, Charles Ulm, and their navigators, made the first flight from America to Australia in a Fokker tri-motor. They refueled four times on Pacific islands. The first round-the-world solo flight was made between July 15 and 22, 1933. Total flying time was 7 days, 18 hours, and 49 minutes for the 15,596 miles. The pilot was an American called Wiley Post, and his aircraft was a Lockheed Vega.

Fokker tri-motor

15

SAILING THE SEAS

People have used boats for thousands of years. A simple "logboat" can be made by hollowing out a tree trunk. Pictures on vases show that Egyptians were building ships with sails by 3,500 BC.

Corsair

Ancient Greek galley

Mayflower

A Corsair's galley
Corsairs were pirates in the Mediterranean about 400 years ago. They sailed in galleys rowed by slaves.

Rowing into battle
Ancient Greek warships were called galleys. Slaves rowed while soldiers fought on deck. Galleys had a sharp ram at the bow (front) to sink enemy ships.

Galleons
Galleons were used for trading and fighting in the 1600s. The first pilgrims sailed to America in the galleon Mayflower, in 1620.

Telescopes
Hans Lippershey, a Dutch spectacles maker, probably made the first telescope in 1608. The lens (curved piece of glass) at the front end of a telescope gathers light to make an image of a distant object. The rear lens magnifies the image so that it can be seen more clearly.

Hans Lippershey

Cutaway of telescope

Clippers

Whalers

Hunting whales
Whales were once hunted for oil and meat. Once sighted the whalers threw or fired long spears (harpoons) at each whale to kill it.

Clippers
Clippers were fast-sailing cargo ships. Built in America and Europe in the 19th century, they carried important cargoes, such as tea from China, quickly around the world.

16

Pyroscaphe

Astrolabe

The first steamboat
The first steamboat was called Pyroscaphe. It was built in France and had two paddle wheels. In 1783 it worked for just 15 minutes before it fell apart because of the thumping movement of the engines.

Tug of war
In 1845, two British naval steamships had a tug of war, to see if propellers were better than paddles for making a ship move through the water. HMS Rattler, with a propeller, pulled HMS Alecto, which had paddles, backwards at a speed of three knots.

Chinese boats
Chinese sailors have been going to sea in ships called junks for more than a thousand years. Large junks have cloth sails with five bamboo masts.

Chinese junk

Navigating the oceans
An astrolabe had two discs, one with a star map, and the other with measuring lines and a pointer. Sailors compared the discs with the Sun or a star and the horizon to work out their position.

HMS Rattler   HMS Alecto

Pirate attack

Chinese boat

Fire the cannons!

Pirates
The skull and crossbones was the flag of pirates, who flew it from their ships. Pirates attacked ships, especially in the Mediterranean and Caribbean. They often killed the crew, stole the cargo, and sometimes the ship itself!

Pirate flag

Bonny and Read

Bonny and Read
Mary Read and Anne Bonny were a famous pirate team. Read ran away to sea disguised as a boy and Bonny joined a pirate ship aged 16. They met when Bonny's ship captured Read's.

BENEATH THE WAVES

The first diving helmets were borrowed from suits of armor. Air was pumped to the diver on the sea bed through a leather hose pipe. If he fell over, his helmet filled with water and he drowned!

Alvin and Jason Junior
Alvin is a submersible that carries a crew of three. Jason Junior is a robot submersible that can be operated from Alvin or from a ship on the surface. In 1985, Jason Junior discovered the wreck of the ocean liner HMS Titanic at the bottom of the Atlantic Ocean.

Junior Jason

Alvin

Micro sub
A micro sub (also called a submersible) is a small submarine, often used for exploring under the sea.

Micro sub

Underwater land
There are mountains, volcanoes, and valleys on the sea bed, just as there are on dry land. The Mid-Atlantic Ridge is a long line of underwater mountains in the Atlantic Ocean. Steep underwater valleys are known as trenches.

Deep sea submersible
Extra-strong-hulled subs called bathyscaphes can dive many miles under the sea. In 1960, Trieste made the deepest dive ever–an incredible 35,797 feet into the Marianas Trench.

Trieste

Rubbish tip
Every day thousands of tons of garbage are thrown into the sea. The sea bed is littered with it.

Dumping garbage at sea

First Submarine
Built in 1776 the first sub was called Turtle. A person sat inside and pedaled to make its propellers turn.

Turtle

Volcanic island chain

Undersea volcano

Hitching a ride
The biggest fish is also one of the most harmless. The whale shark is 49 feet long and weighs about 13 tons. These gentle giants have been known to allow scuba divers to hang on to their fins and ride with them.

Whale shark and diver

Building coral reefs
Huge coral reefs are built by tiny sea creatures called polyps. They build hard, stony cases around their soft bodies. When they die, the cases are left behind. Millions and millions make a coral reef.

Underwater peak
The highest mountain on Earth from base to peak isn't Mt Everest. It's Mauna Kea in the Pacific. This huge, underwater mountain is 33,474 feet tall.

Basking shark

Coral reef

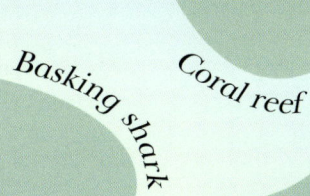

Exploring the depths

Swimming with dolphins

Ray

Sunbathing shark
Basking sharks spend much of their time wallowing at the ocean's surface, especially when it's sunny–probably because there's more food there on sunny days, not because they want a suntan!

Rays and skates
Rays and skates are related to sharks. They all have skeletons made of rubbery cartilage.

Speedy seal
The fastest seal in the sea is the California sea lion, with a top speed of 25 mph.

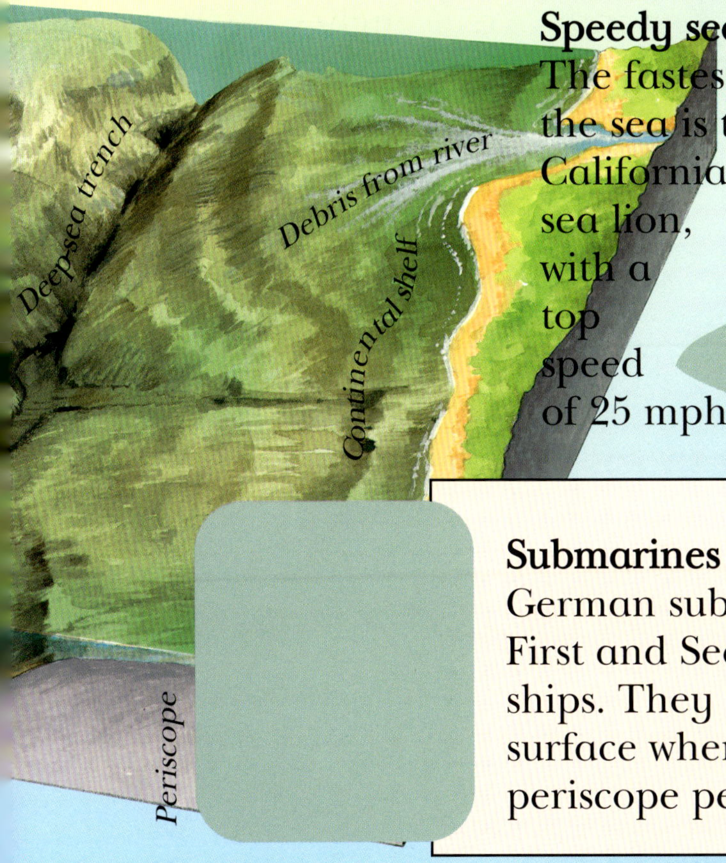

Friendly dolphins
Dolphins are very friendly. People love to swim and play games with them. Submarines use the same sort of sonar as dolphins. The sonar machine makes beeps of sound that spread out through the water. When an object is detected, the sound bounces back to the submarine. The machine works out how big and how far away it is.

Deep sea trench *Debris from river* *Continental shelf* *Seal* *German U-boat*

Periscope

Submarines
German submarines used in the First and Second World Wars sank thousands of ships. They used their periscopes to see ships on the surface when they were submerged. The top of the periscope peeps out above the surface of the water.

19

OCEAN LIFE

Sharks are fish. They breathe through gills and are cold blooded. Whales and dolphins are warm-blooded mammals. Big mammals are better able to keep warm in the freezing oceans than smaller ones.

Commerson's

Gulf porpoises

Harp seal pup

Seal pups
Harp seal pups are born with soft, white fur coats. They lose them after a month and grow dark coats like adult seals. In the past, thousands of pups were killed for their fur.

The tiniest whale
The miniature Commerson's dolphin is about three feet long. It takes about 3,000 of them to make up the weight of one blue whale.

The largest turtle
The leatherback turtle is about the size of a small car. This giant reptile can grow to almost ten feet from nose to tail and also across its front flippers. It can weigh almost a ton.

Rare sea mammal
There may be only 50 Gulf porpoises left off the Californian coast.

Camouflaged killers
The killer whale's black and white coloring could be camouflage, helping to hide it in the light and shade near the surface of the water. It can then surprise its prey.

Living in a pod
Some dolphins live in family groups called pods. A pod can contain hundreds of dolphins. The dolphins help each other out.

Leatherback turtle

Killer whales

Pod of dolphins

Blue whale and calf

Big babies
When a baby blue whale is born, it weighs between two and three tons. It drinks about 350 pints of its mother's milk a day, and by seven months old, it weighs about 20 tons!

Dugong

Walrus

Vegetarian mammals
Only manatees and dugongs are vegetarians. They feed on sea grasses and other sea plants. All other sea mammals eat meat, or other creatures of some kind.

Walrus tusks
A walrus uses its long tusks to chip shellfish from rocks and break breathing holes in the ice.

Humpback whale

Out in the cold
Weddell seals live in the far south, on ice-covered islands off the coast of freezing Antarctica. Ringed seals live in the Arctic, at the other end of the world.

Weddell seal

Trapping fish
Humpbacks, killer whales, and dolphins swim around shoals of fish, blowing bubbles from their blowholes. Then they swim and gobble up the trapped fish!

Differences
Strictly speaking, dolphins are small whales with sharp, pointed teeth for catching food. They live in seas all over the world. The biggest dolphin is the killer whale.

Polar bear

Walking on ice
Polar bears roam across northern Europe, northern Asia, and northern North America. If the Arctic Ocean isn't frozen they swim, protected by thick fur and fat!

Red balloon
To attract a mate or scare off a rival, a male hooded seal blows air into its nose! It can inflate the lining of one of its nostrils so that it looks like a big, red balloon.

Hooded seal

Dolphin

Blue whale

Herding fish
When dolphins are hunting for anchovy, they herd the fish towards the surface, giving them less chance to escape. They also make loud noises to confuse the fish, making them easier to catch.

Dolphins hunting fish

The biggest sea mammal
The huge blue whale can grow to more than 98 feet long and weigh as much as 130 tons.

FABULOUS STUFF

The first Europeans to cross the Atlantic Ocean were probably Vikings. In the 9th century, the voyage from Iceland to Canada would have taken three weeks. Modern supersonic aircraft can do it in three hours!

Splashdown
When capsules re-entered Earth's atmosphere at 18,750 mph, they got extremely hot. A heat shield protected the crew from 3,000° C temperatures outside. Then they splashed down into the cold sea.

Satellites
When satellites crash, they often fall into the ocean. However, some pieces of the empty space station Skylab were found on farmland in Australia, after it fell back to Earth in 1979.

Hollowed out logs
Ancient people made boats called dugout canoes by hollowing out large tree trunks.

Capsule entering Earth's atmosphere

Satellite crashing into the ocean

Amy Johnson

Dugongs

Gypsy Moth

Sailors waving to mermaids

Dugout canoe

England to Australia
English pilot Amy Johnson made the first solo England to Australia flight by a woman, in a Gypsy Moth biplane in 1930. She had many near disasters on the way, including almost flying into a mountainside.

Mermaids
Legends of mysterious mermaids may have started with a dugong. Close-to, dugongs don't look anything like mermaids, but from a distance, and in a sea mist, they are shaped a bit like humans, complete with fish-like tails. Manatees and dugongs live in tropical rivers and in warm, shallow water near the coast, in tropical seas.

Rocket pieces

Rockets are made in stages, or pieces. Usually, there are three stages, made up of the fuel and rocket engines. Each stage drops off as its job is done. It then falls to Earth and crashes in to the ocean.

Solo flight

American pilot Charles Lindbergh made the first nonstop transatlantic solo flight in 1927. His monoplane was built specially for the job. The flight took 33 hours and 30 minutes.

Ryan M2 monoplane Spirit of St Louis

First across the Atlantic

Britons John Alcock and Arthur Brown flew across the Atlantic in 1919. It took 16 hours and 17 minutes and ended with a crash into a bog.

Migrating geese

Rocket stages falling away

Tornado at sea

Giant waterspouts can twist up to a height of almost a mile sucking up tons of water from the sea. In the past, sailors thought they were sea monsters!

Dugong and manatee

It's all in the tail

You can tell manatees and dugongs apart by the shape of their tails. A manatee's tail is round. A dugong's tail is pointed like a dolphin's.

Asleep on a seabed

Florida manatees don't have homes on land, so they sleep on the seabed. They have to surface every ten minutes to breathe.

Vickers Vimy bomber

Splashdown of capsule

Migrating across the world

Geese migrate together. The younger birds learn which way to go by following the older birds in front.

Waterspout

Manatees are known as sea cows

Parachuting into the ocean

Once the air slowed a capsule down, the astronauts inside released large parachutes. These acted as giant brakes, letting the capsule land softly on water. Once landed, the astronauts could be picked up by helicopter. All the Moonwalking astronauts splashed down at sea.

23

THE SOLAR SYSTEM

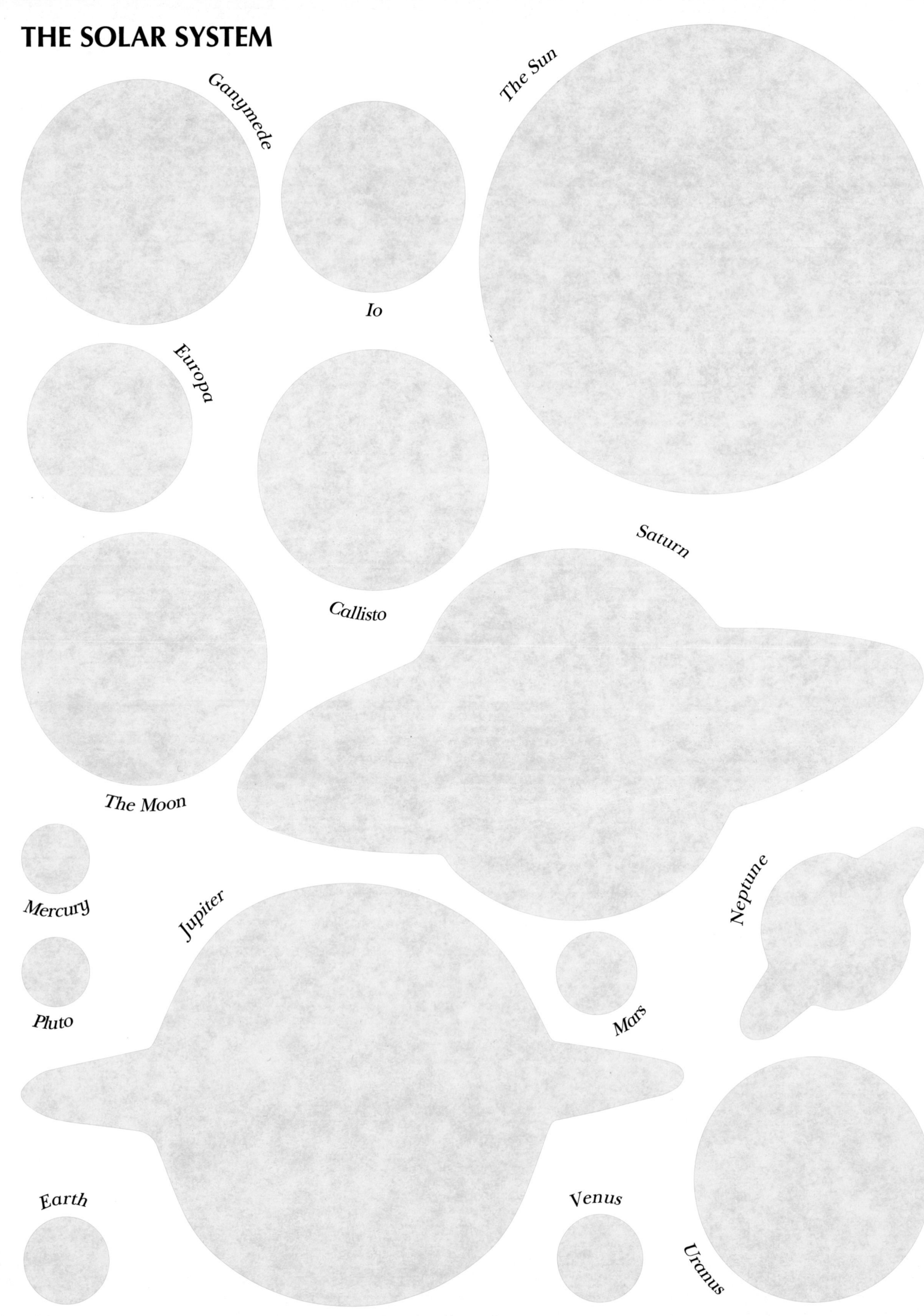

MAN IN SPACE

International Space Station

Yuri Gagarin

Space suit

V2 missile

Saturn 5 rocket

Valentina Tereshkova

Lunar Rover

MMU

Buzz Aldrin

Neil Armstrong

Space shuttle

Mercury capsule

Space shuttle and Mir

Laika

Wernher von Braun

SAILING THE SEAS

Mayflower

Pyroscaphe

Chinese boat

Hans Lippershey

HMS Rattler   HMS Alecto

Fire the cannons!

Corsair

Pirate flag

Whalers

Chinese junk

Bonny and Read

Pirate attack

Ancient Greek galley

Astrolabe

Cutaway of telescope

OCEAN LIFE

Blue whale

Commerson's

Harp seal pup

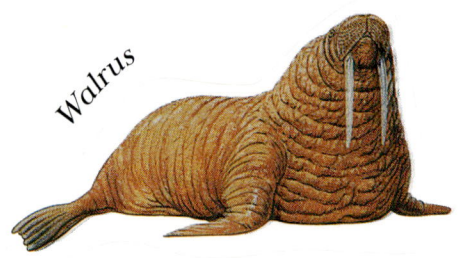
Walrus

Polar bear

Humpback whale

Dolphin

Dugong

Killer whales

Weddell seal

Hooded seal

Gulf porpoises

Dolphins hunting fish

Leatherback turtle

Blue whale and calf

FABULOUS STUFF

Satellite crashing into the ocean

Rocket stages falling away

Dugout canoe

Gypsy Moth

Migrating geese

Ryan M2 monoplane
Spirit of St Louis

Sailors waving to mermaids

Splashdown of capsule

Manatees are known as sea cows

Dugong and manatee

Vickers Vimy bomber

Waterspout

Capsule entering Earth's atmosphere
Amy Johnson

Dugongs

BENEATH THE WAVES

Junior Jason

Periscope

Whale shark and diver

Coral reef

Exploring the depths

Seal

Basking shark

Alvin

Turtle

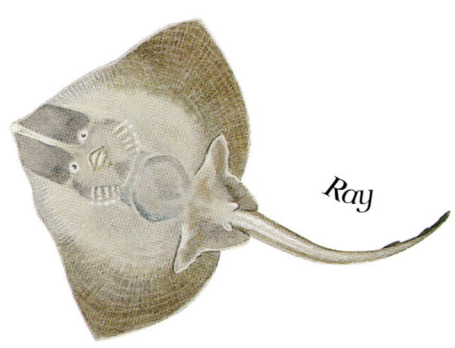
Ray

German U-boat

Dumping garbage at sea

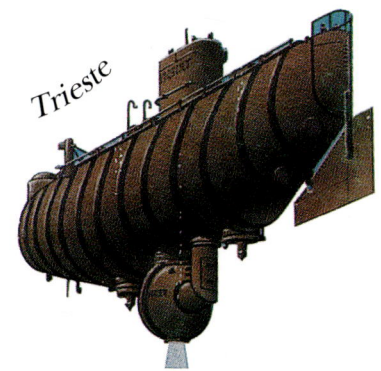
Trieste

Swimming with dolphins

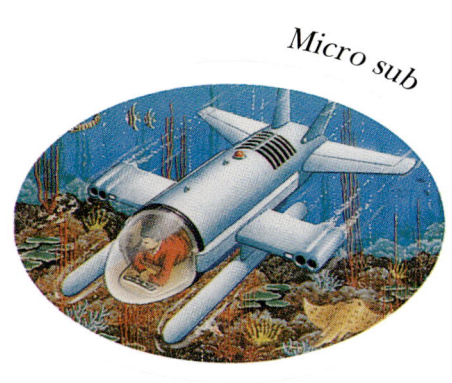
Micro sub

EXPLORING SPACE

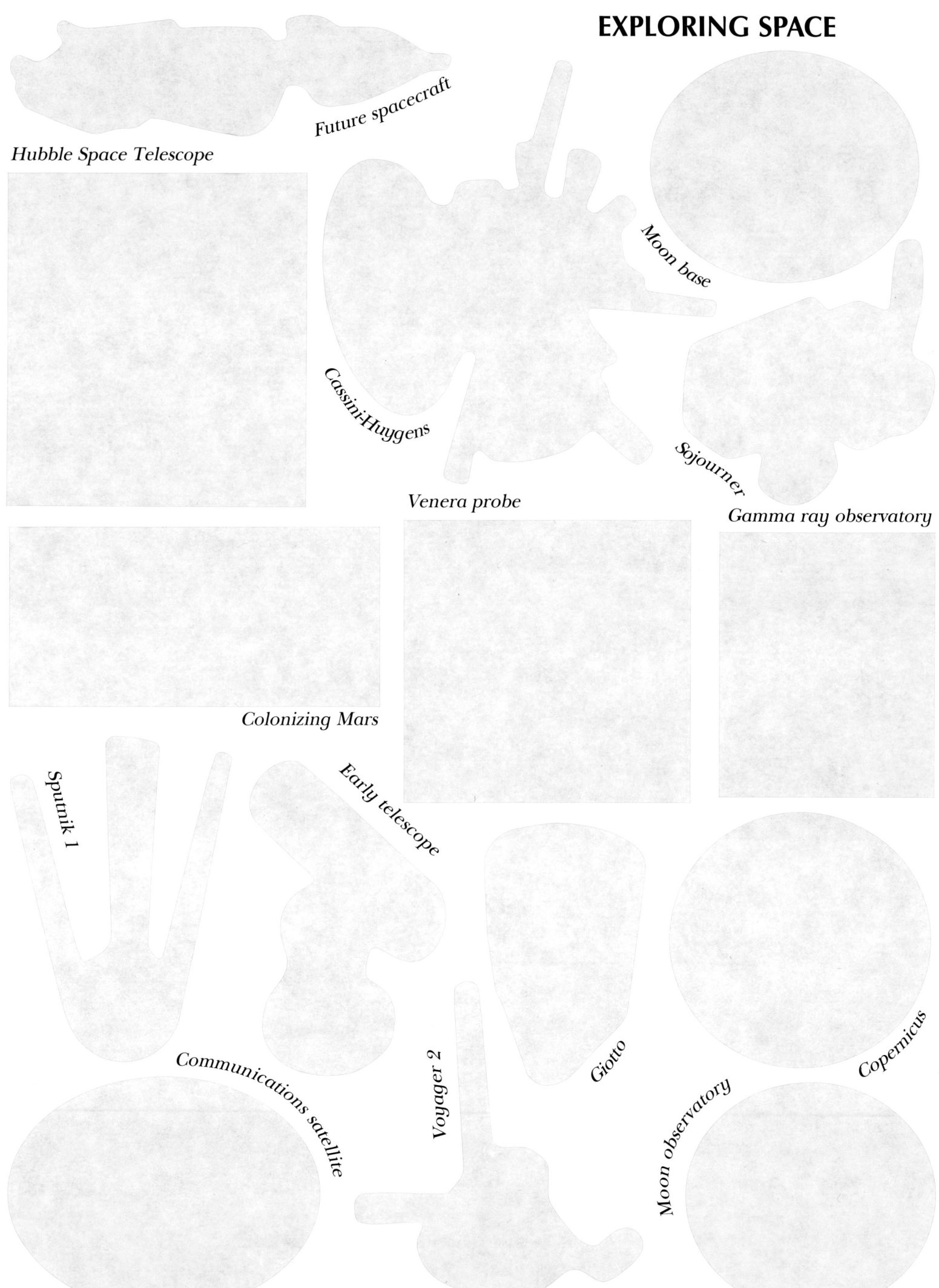

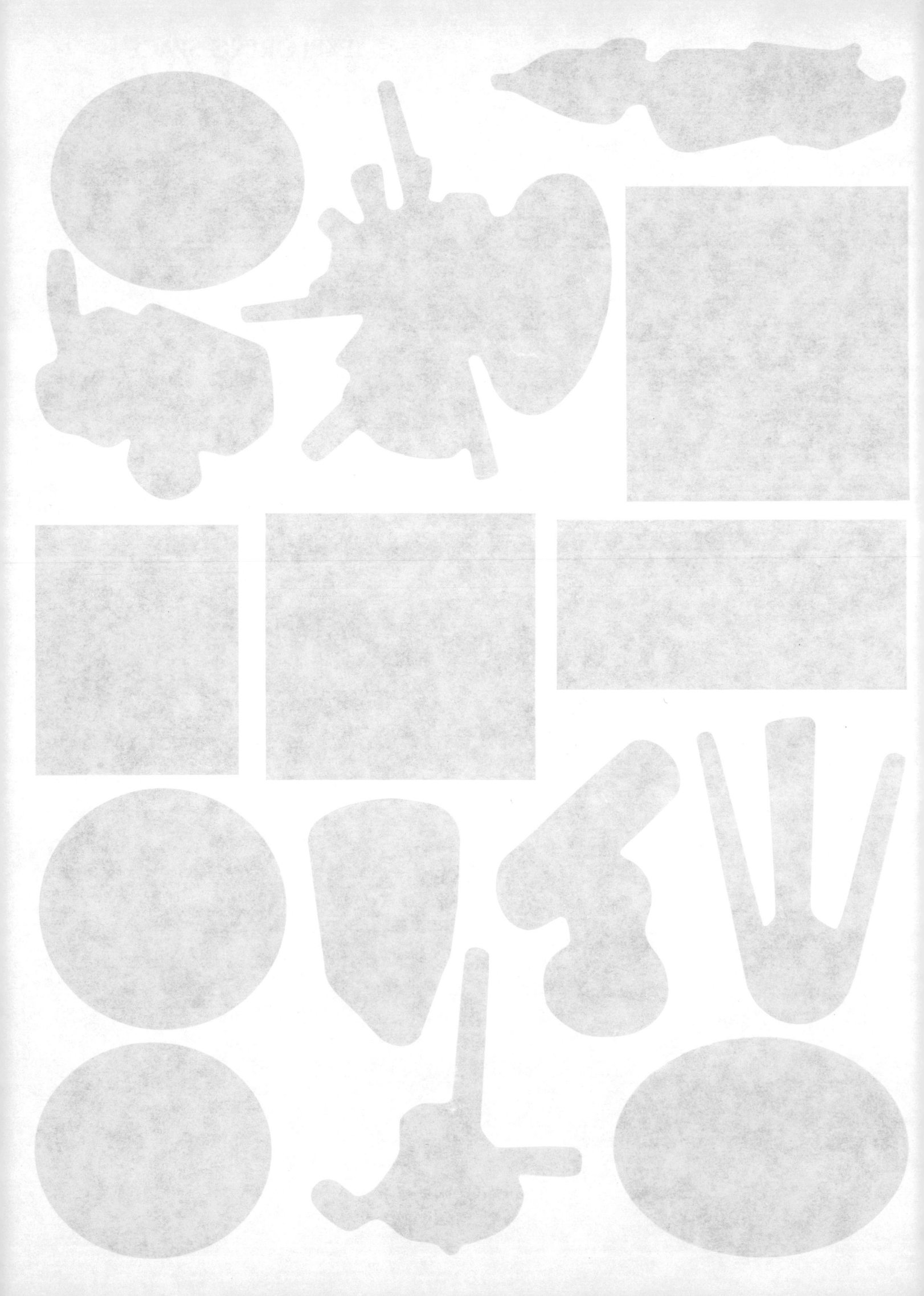

OUTER SPACE

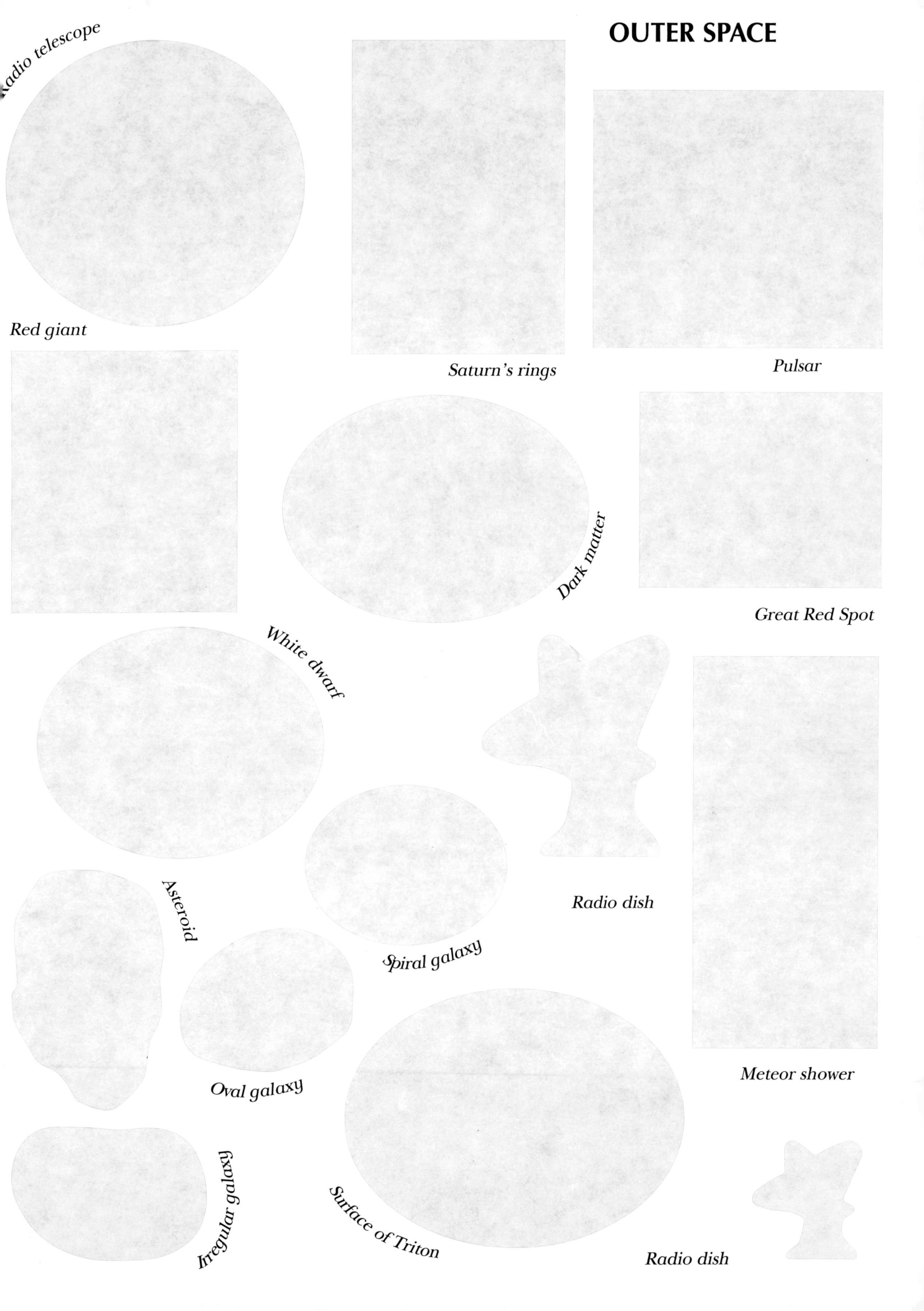

Radio telescope

Red giant

Saturn's rings

Pulsar

White dwarf

Dark matter

Great Red Spot

Asteroid

Spiral galaxy

Radio dish

Oval galaxy

Meteor shower

Irregular galaxy

Surface of Triton

Radio dish

CHANGING PLANET

Shooting stars

Mudslide survivors are rescued by helicopter in Armero, Colombia

Spreading desert

El Nino represented by red areas along the center of Earth

Freezing temperatures

Hikers

Ball lightning

Duststorm during the Midwest USA heatwave, 1937

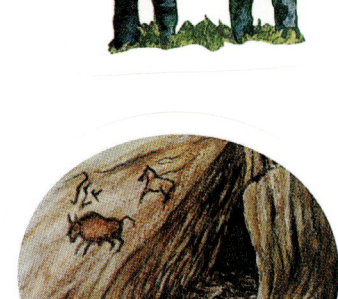

Cave art

Coastal cliffs

Interior of Earth

Firefighters battle a large wildfire

People caught in a flood

Soil erosion on Madagascar seen from space

Glacier shedding ice in Antarctic

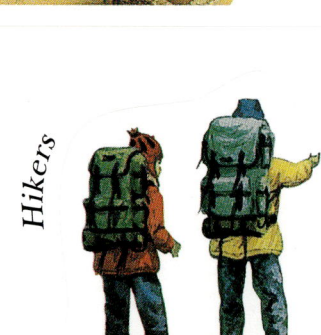

EARTH MANAGEMENT

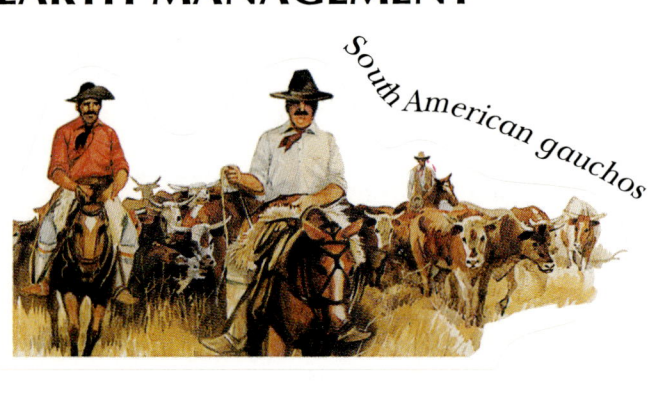

South American gauchos

Rainforest layers

Pole
Sun's rays
Equator

Hoover Dam, USA

Endangered animals

Lake Superior

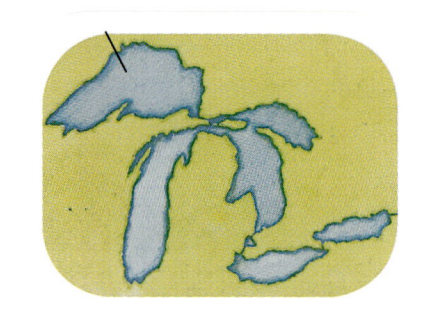

Salt farms

Lake Titicaca

Flooded river

Furnace

Great Lakes

Urban foxes

Wind power

Organic farming

River Nile in flood

LIVING LANDSCAPES

Coniferous forest

Mammoth caves

Rainforest plants and animals

North Pole

The life of a river

Desert landscapes

Shrinking mountain

South Pole

Greenland

A coral island

African savannah (grassland)

Glacier

The Amazon river

Limestone cave system

Lake-forming landscapes

AMAZING WEATHER

Leaving a trail of damage

Record-breaking hailstone

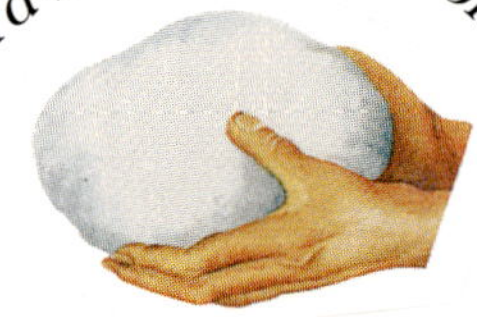

Cliffs worn by waves

Flash flood, Ouveze River, France

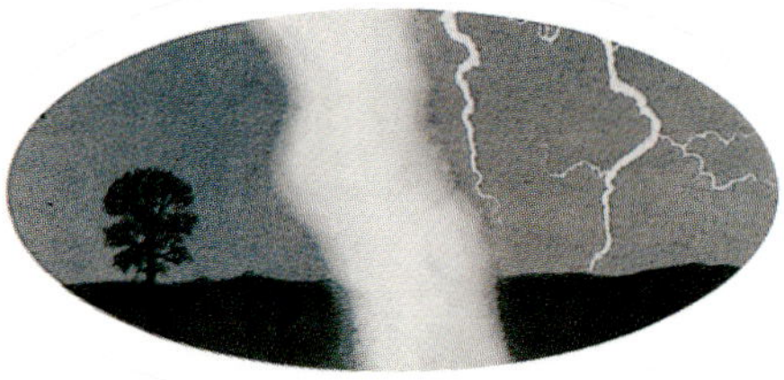

Geyser in Yellowstone Park, USA

Build-up of hailstone in thundercloud

Lightning strike

Boat stranded inland

Cutaway of a hurricane

Volcano erupting

Sandstorm in Africa

Sand dunes covering a town

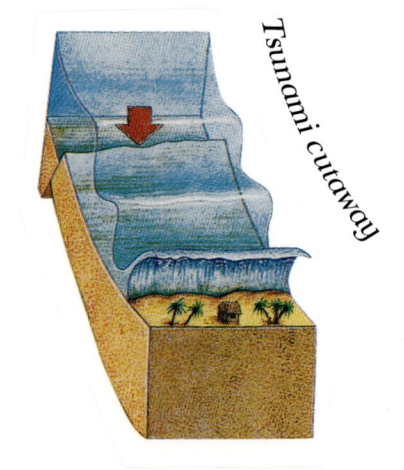

Tsunami cutaway

Battling against a blizzard

Eye of hurricane seen from space

OTHER PLANETS

Saturn and Earth

Mercury and Earth

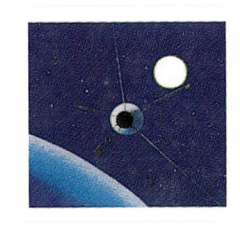

Voyager probe passing Neptune

Side of Milky Way galaxy seen from deep space

Cassini probe carrying the Huygens probe to Titan

Alien life?

Radio astronomy centre

Jupiter and Earth

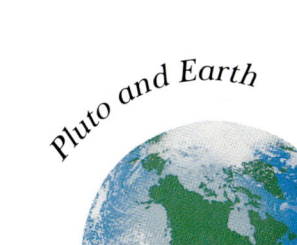

Radio telescopes

Venus and Earth

Uranus and Earth

Moon Base

Neptune

Mars and Earth

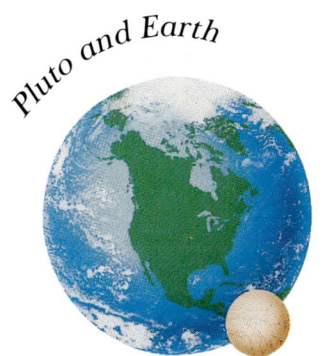

Pluto and Earth

DESTRUCTIVE EARTH

Avalanche

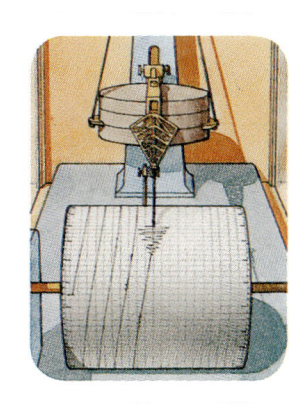

Seismograph (earthquake measuring device)

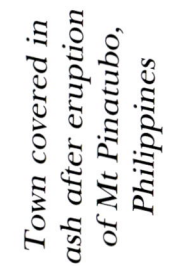

Earth's main continental plates

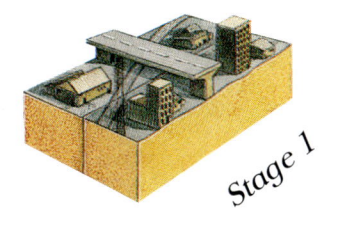

Stage 1

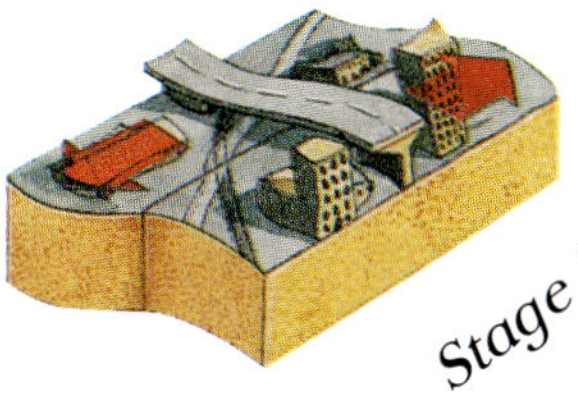

Town covered in ash after eruption of Mt Pinatubo, Philippines

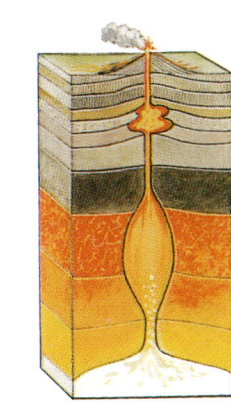

Stage 2

Landslide

Cliff collapsing into the sea

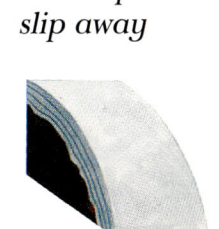

Cross-section of a Volcano

Layers of snow and ice build up then slip away

Mt St Helen's, USA was a dormant volcano that erupted

Pompeii, AD 79

Kobe earthquake, Japan, 1995

Stage 3

WHAT CAN I DO?

- Reused plastic bottles
- Recycling center 
- Tomato growing  
- Sunbathers 
- Green club 
- Illegal animal goods 
- Sorting garbage 
- Greenhouse 
- Compost can be made from some kinds of paper 
- Using magnets to test cans 
- Gardener
- Reusing cloths
- Cans
- Biogas plant in India
- Paper recycling

GLOBAL DAMAGE

Crop spraying

Cormorant covered in oil

Nuclear storage

Dustbowl

Shark fishing

Golden lion tamarin

Logging truck

Collecting rainforest plants

Polluted river

Climate study in the Antarctic

Corn crop

Oil spill

Garbage dump

Cars and factories

People

STICKER BOOKS
OUR INCREDIBLE WORLD

WORLD OF WONDERS

From the deepest jungles to the most barren deserts, our incredible world is full of amazing sights. From a distance all looks well. But get closer, and you see a different picture. Parts of the Earth are unhealthy–because of the way people live. Looking after the world to make sure it stays a beautiful, healthy place, shared by everyone, is very important.

Rainforest

Coral island seen from above

An island paradise
A coral island begins life as a coral reef. It grows around the top of an underwater volcano that sticks out from the sea. When the volcano sank into the sea, it left a horseshoe, or ring-shaped coral island behind.

Precious rainforests
Forests are the "lungs" of the planet. Their trees make much of the oxygen we breathe. Forests provide us with food and timber. Some medicines are made from plants found only in forests.

Storm chasers observing a tornado in Kansas, USA

Fascinating tornadoes
A tornado is a fierce, twisting wind that hangs from a thundercloud. It starts when wind inside the cloud starts to spin very quickly. A twisty tornado speeds across the ground, sucking up everything in its way. Some people track tornadoes for fun. They drive as close to the twister as they dare, then take video films and photos. It's a very dangerous hobby!

Angel Falls

Wonderful waterfalls
The highest waterfall in the world is Angel Falls in Venezuela. It plunges 3212 feet down the side of a mountain. Angel Falls is 20 times higher than the famous Niagara Falls in North America.

Sandy desert seen from above

Beautiful deserts
Deserts are the driest places on Earth. In some deserts it doesn't rain for years at a time. In others, it never rains at all. Some deserts are also scorching hot. In the daytime, the sand's hot enough to fry an egg on. The Sahara Desert is the biggest, sandiest desert in the world. It covers about a third of Africa.

27

CHANGING PLANET

Earth is around 4.5 billion years old. In that time, it has seen a lot of change; the rise and fall of the dinosaurs, for example. In recent centuries, human beings have also made their mark.

People caught in a flood

Soil erosion
Trees keep soil in place. Where forests are cleared, the soil wears away, or erodes, until only rock is left.

Soil erosion on Madagascar seen from space

Shooting stars
A shooting star, or meteor, happens when a tiny space rock, called a meteoroid, enters Earth's atmosphere and burns up.

El Niño
El Niño is a warm band of water that flows in the sea. Scientists blame El Niño for changing the weather, by causing more storms, floods, droughts, and tornadoes.

Ball lightning

Shooting stars

Interior of Earth

El Niño represented by red areas along the center of Earth

Ball lightning
People have seen balls of lightning float into their house, then explode with a bang.

Temperature rise
As the Earth's climate warms up, droughts will occur and deserts will spread.

Inside the Earth
The Earth is made up of layers of rock and metal. We live on the hard surface, called the crust. Below, the layers are so hot that they've melted and turned runny. At the center is a ball of metal.

Spreading desert

Hikers

Thunderstorms
Thunder usually happens on hot, summer days when the air is warm and sticky. It starts in huge cumulonimbus clouds which turn the sky purply black and can be over 11 miles high.

Carving the cliffs
Along the coast, the rocks are worn away by the force of the waves. As the waves crash against the shore, they carve out cliffs, caves, and high arches. Sometimes an arch collapses, leaving a stack, or pillar, of rock.

Coastal cliffs

Underground art galleries
Thousands of years ago, prehistoric people sheltered in caves and painted pictures on the walls. The best underground art gallery is in the Lascaux Caves in France. The walls are covered with hundreds of animals, including bison and mammoths.

Cave art

Rising sea levels
The Antarctic ice sheet holds two thirds of the Earth's fresh water. If it melted, the sea would rise by up to 230 feet. Coastlines would change all over the world.

Glacier shedding ice in Antarctic

Firefighters battle a large wildfire

Wildfires
Wildfires destroy huge patches of forest and spread very quickly, especially in dry weather. Most fires are started by people to clear space for farms. They can easily get out of control.

Freezing!
The coldest place on Earth is Vostok in Antarctica. Here temperatures can plummet to minus 190°F.

Freezing temperatures

Duststorm during the Midwest USA heatwave, 1937

Heatwaves and mudslides
In very hot weather heatwaves that can kill people, animals, and crops can develop. They dry up reservoirs and rivers. In 1985, a volcano erupted in Colombia, South America. It melted masses of snow and ice, which turned soil into a mudslide. It poured down the hillside and buried a whole town.

Mudslide survivors are rescued by helicopter in Armero, Colombia

GLOBAL DAMAGE

Crop spraying

A hundred years ago, the population of the world was around 1.5 billion. Today, there are four times that number. Feeding, clothing, and sheltering so many takes a heavy toll on our fragile planet.

Climate study in the Antarctic

Changing climate
Earth's climate is slowly getting warmer. Scientists who study the climate have found that it is a little warmer now than it was 100 years ago. You may not notice the difference, but plants and animals do. By burning "fossil fuels"–coal, oil, and natural gas–we are putting "greenhouse gases," such as carbon dioxide, into the atmosphere. The gases surround the Earth and keep heat in.

Cars and factories

People power
It's getting warmer because of the way people are leading their lives.

People

Nuclear power
Nuclear power stations do not burn fossil fuels and so do not make harmful gases. They make radioactive waste material. It is dangerous and will have to be stored for many years into the future.

Nuclear storage

River pollution
Green waste in a garbage dump makes dangerous methane gas and liquid that can pollute water and kill wildlife. It's safer to make it into compost.

Polluted river

Crop spraying
Spraying crops with chemicals can harm the delicate balance of nature.

Dustbowls
In the 1930s, farmers in southwest USA plowed up the grasslands to grow wheat. But a terrible drought turned the soil to dry, useless dust that blew away in the wind. This was called a dustbowl.

So much garbage!
People make garbage and every household makes lots of it every day. The world's garbage mountain grows by about 2 million tons every day.

Garbage dump

Shark fishing
People kill millions of sharks every year, some to protect swimmers, others for food or just for sport. If too many are killed, sharks might disappear altogether.

Shark fishing

Endangered species
Some animals and plants are so rare they are endangered. This means they are almost extinct– they have almost died out. If that happens, they will have gone forever.

Golden lion tamarin

Taken away
Every year around 100 million animals and plants are taken without permission from the wild. It is because of this that they are endangered.

Collecting rainforest plants

Dustbowl

Forests in danger
Forests are in danger in many parts of the world. Acid rain, which is produced by sulphur dioxide from power stations and vehicles, kills trees.

Logging truck

GM foods
Some people are worried about genetically modified (GM) foods. No one yet knows if they are safe.

Corn crop

Animals in danger
Thousands of different animals live on Earth. It is their planet, as well as ours. Sadly, because of what we do, many animals are in danger. An oil spill at sea harms seals, birds, and fish. When forests are cut down, many animals lose their homes.

Oil spill

Cormorant covered in oil

EARTH MANAGEMENT

Good hunters, farmers and fishermen know they must look after the forests, fields, and oceans that feed the world. But people do not always find it easy to share a planet.

"Organic farming"
It's a natural way of farming. Crops are grown and animals are raised without using manmade chemicals. Also, the plants and animals have not been changed in any way.

Organic farming

River Nile in flood

Wind power

Flooded river

Floods
Many floods happen when it rains very heavily. Rivers burst their banks and flood the land all around. Some floods are good. The River Nile in Egypt used to flood every year, leaving rich mud on the fields. The mud made the soil ideal for farmers to grow bumper crops.

Pole
Sun's rays
Equator

The Poles
The Poles are the coldest places on Earth. They are cold because the Sun's rays hit them at a slant, so they're spread out and very weak.

Clean energy
The spinning propellers of wind turbines collect energy from the wind. Solar power, wind power, and bio-gas are cleaner, or "green," forms of energy. They don't pollute the atmosphere, make acid rain, or harm the ozone layer.

Hoover Dam, USA

Electricity from water
Running water is used to make electricity. This is hydroelectric power. The electricity is produced by power stations built in or near dams.

South American gauchos

Grasslands
People use grasslands for grazing animals such as cattle which are raised for their meat. They also grow crops such as wheat and barley in gigantic fields. One wheat field in Canada was the size of 20,000 soccer pitches.

Controlling garbage
Because so much garbage is made, it's a problem to deal with it all. Some is burned inside furnaces. A lot is buried underground and some is recycled.

Saving animals
Many endangered animals are now protected by law. It is wrong for people to harm them or the places where they live. Some are bred in zoos to increase their numbers.

Studying the rainforests
Scientists study the rainforests to help protect them. The rainforests have a number of layers. The tallest trees poke out above the forest. Below them is a thick roof of treetops called the canopy. Next comes a layer of shorter trees, herbs, and shrubs.

Freshwater lake
The biggest freshwater lake on Earth is Lake Superior in North America. It covers 31,795 square miles. Lake Superior is one of five huge lakes called the Great Lakes.

Great Lakes

Lake Superior

Collecting salt
The sea's salty taste comes from the same ordinary salt that is sprinkled on food. The rain washes the salt out of rocks on land, then rivers carry it into the sea. People collect salt left after sea water dries.

Living by a lake
Lake Titicaca in South America is 12,500 feet up in the Andes Mountains. People who live around the lake build boats from lake reeds.

At home in the city
The British red fox is just as happy in the town as in the countryside. During the night, it goes through garbage cans looking for tasty morsels or it catches rats.

Urban foxes

WHAT CAN I DO?

Human beings have created most of the problems facing the world, so it's up to human beings to solve them. It's easy to feel there is nothing one person can do to help: in fact, there's plenty!

Green club
Join your school's Recycling Club. If it doesn't have one, ask if one can be started.

Recycling club

Recycling cans
Soda cans are often made from aluminum. They can be melted down and made into new cans. Most food cans are made from the world's most recycled material–steel. Take sorted cans to a can bank.

Recycling paper
Most paper can be recycled, from newspapers and telephone directories to candy wrappers and envelopes. It is made into new paper and cardboard.

Grow your own
It's easy, and fun, to grow some foods at home, such as tomatoes. Be organic, so don't put any fertilizers on them. They'll taste good!

Recycling plastic
Some kinds of plastic can be recycled. Soda bottles can eventually be turned into car parts. Bottles can also be reused, by making them into useful items.

Cans

Using magnets to test cans

Paper recycling

Tomato growing

Reused plastic bottles

Energy efficient house

Insulation to keep the heat in

Switch off electrical items after use

Don't leave taps dripping

Grow your own organic vegetables

Cycling is energy efficient and good exercise

Old clothes
Give old clothes to charity shops. They are sorted out and some are sent abroad to help other people.

Old glass
When glass bottles and jars are empty, wash them out and take them to a recycling center.

Reusing clothes

Recycling center

Recycled metal goods

Protect yourself
People are protected from the Sun's dangerous ultraviolet rays by a layer of gas that surrounds Earth called ozone. This layer is damaged because of harmful chemicals in the atmosphere. So always protect your skin by using a sunscreen.

Natural fuels
In many countries small amounts of energy come from rotting plants and animal dung. The methane they give off is burned to provide light and heat. This type of fuel is called bio-gas.

Making a difference
If you would like to make Earth a better, safer place to live, now and in the future, you could join groups such as Greenpeace, Friends of the Earth, or World Wide Fund for Nature. Your library will have their addresses.

Be careful what you buy
Don't buy goods made from ivory, fur, coral, or tortoiseshell. Don't pick or dig up wild plants. If you eat tuna fish, make sure it's dolphin friendly.

Garden waste
Vegetable peelings, tea leaves and grass cuttings are "green" waste. If you pile them into a heap in the garden, they will rot down to make compost.

Sunbathers

Bio-gas plant in India

Sorting garbage

Compost can be made from some kinds of paper

Using compost
Compost is food for the soil. It contains nutrients (foods) that keep soil healthy. Using homemade compost means less peat compost is dug up from natural places, and animals' homes are saved.

Gardener

Greenhouse

35

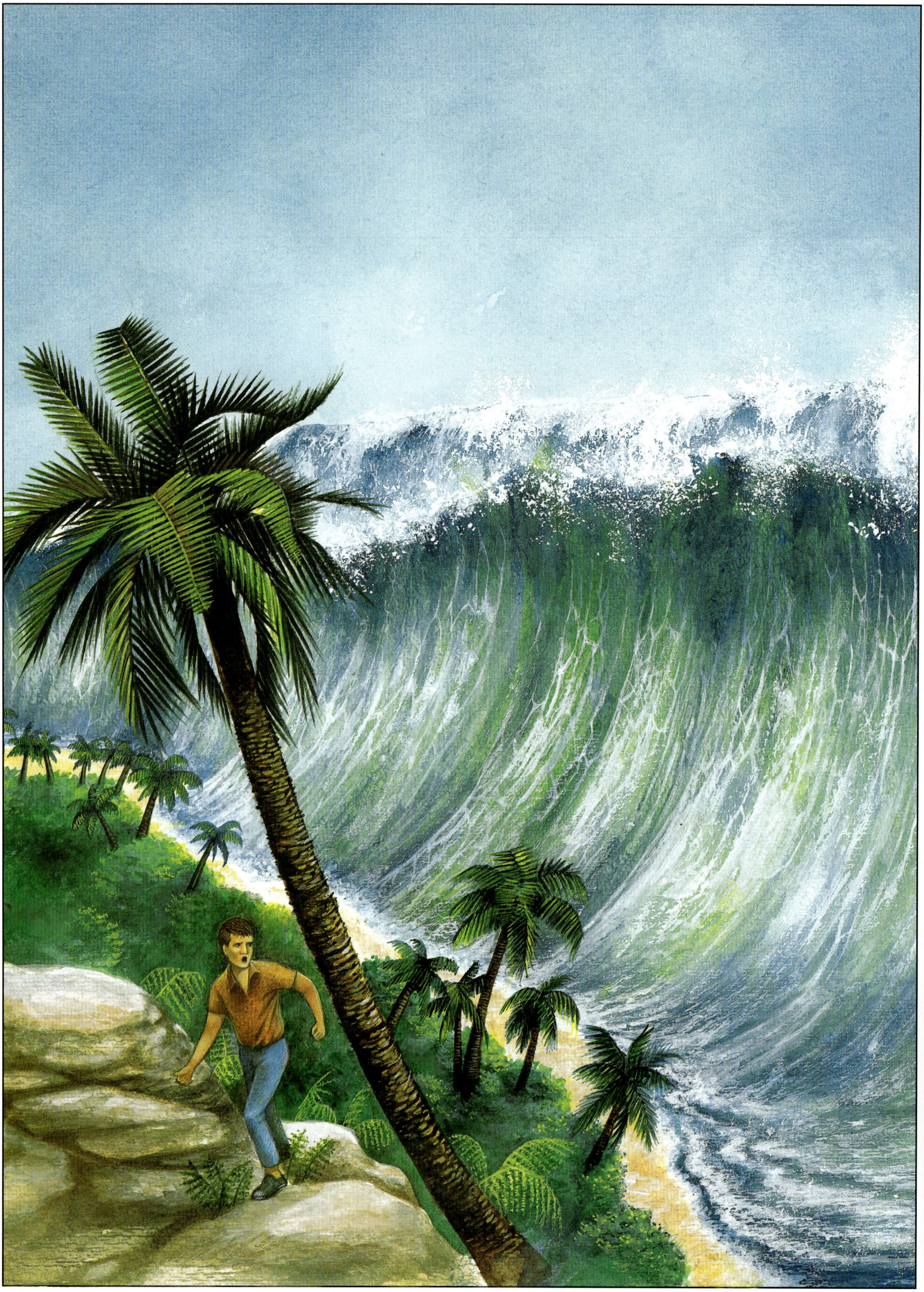

STICKER BOOKS
OUR AMAZING
PLANET

OUR SPECIAL EARTH

The forces of nature that created Earth are very powerful. Look at our planet from space and you see a mainly blue, watery sphere with swirling white clouds. It is very beautiful. There is only one Earth, which makes it a very special place–it is the only planet known to have life on it. Perhaps one day life will be found on another planet, too.

Earth seen from space

Our Solar System has nine planets that orbit the Sun

Reaching up to heaven

The highest mountains in the world are the Himalayas in Asia. This massive mountain range has twelve of the world's 14 highest peaks, including Mt Everest. At 29,029 feet, it's the highest mountain on Earth.

Himalayan mountain range

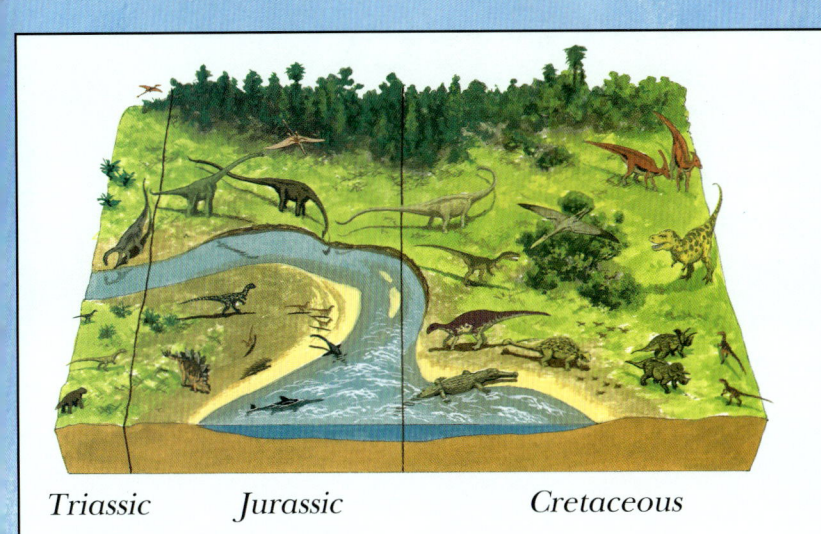

When dinosaurs ruled the world

Dinosaurs appeared about 225 million years ago and died out 65 million years ago. There were three periods in dinosaur history: Triassic, when the first dinosaurs appeared; Jurassic and Cretaceous, when dinosaurs dominated the land.

Triassic   Jurassic   Cretaceous

Making mountains

Some mountains are formed when two pieces of the Earth's crust bump or crash into each other. The rock in between is pushed up into giant fold mountains. Other mountains are formed when huge blocks of rocks are squeezed upward.

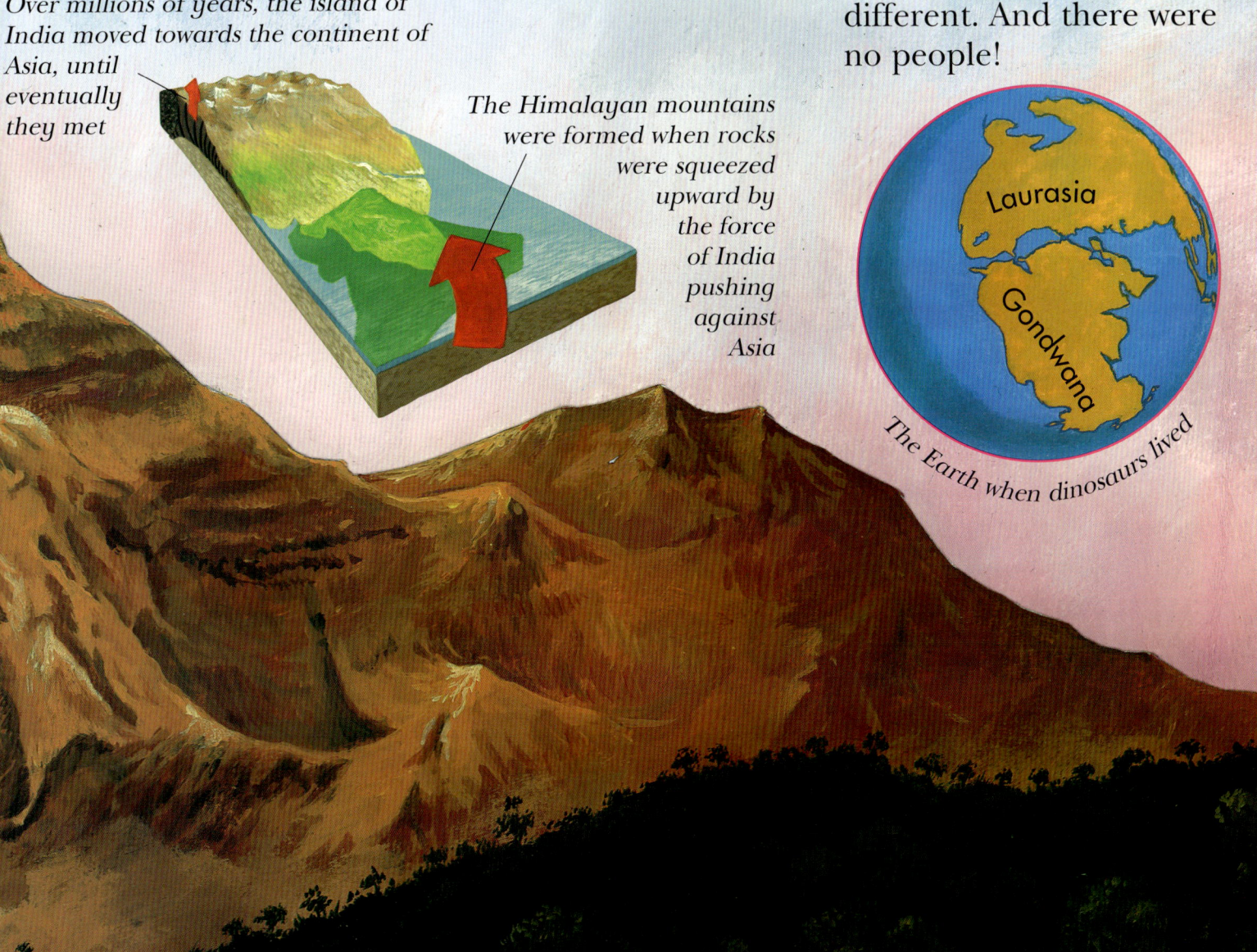

Over millions of years, the island of India moved towards the continent of Asia, until eventually they met

The Himalayan mountains were formed when rocks were squeezed upward by the force of India pushing against Asia

A different world

The planet was completely different in dinosaur times. The seas, plants, animals, and continents–Laurasia and Gondwana–were all different. And there were no people!

Laurasia

Gondwana

The Earth when dinosaurs lived

39

LIVING LANDSCAPES

There are many different landscapes throughout the world. All kinds of plants and animals inhabit them. As the landscape changes, it affects all the creatures living there. Sometimes the changes can take many years and sometimes they can happen in days.

The open savannah
Grasslands (also known as savannah) are huge plains of grass, trees, and bushes. They grow in warm, dry places where there's too little rain for forests to grow, but enough rain to stop the land turning into a desert.

African savannah (grassland)

Northern forests
Huge forests stretch for thousands of miles across northern Europe and Asia. The trees that grow here are conifers.

Coniferous forest

Rainforest plants and animals

Rainforests
Rainforests grow along the Equator where it's hot and sticky all year round. It rains almost every single day! It's the perfect weather for exotic plants and animals. They thrive!

Rivers of ice
Glaciers are enormous rivers of ice that slowly flow down the sides of mountains. The longest glacier in the world is over 373 miles. About a tenth of the Earth is covered in icy glaciers.

Glacier

North Pole

South Pole

Poles of ice
The North and South Poles are at either end of the Earth. The North Pole is surrounded by the frozen Arctic Ocean. The South Pole is in the middle of icy Antarctica.

Greenland

Islands of ice
An island is a chunk of land with water all around it. The biggest island is Greenland, in the icy Arctic Ocean. It measures more than 727,000 square miles.

Under the earth
Deep down beneath many mountains is a secret world of tunnels and caves. Caves are carved out by rainwater trickling through cracks in the ground.

Mammoth caves

Limestone cave system

Mammoth caves
The Mammoth Caves in Kentucky are the longest caves on Earth. They stretch for 348 miles. The biggest single cave is the Sarawak Chamber in Malaysia. Its floor is the size of 30 football pitches.

Lakes
Some lakes formed long ago, in hollows scraped out by ice. These filled with water as the ice melted. Some lakes form in the tops of volcanoes or when a river cuts through a bend.

Lake-forming landscapes

Mountains
It takes millions of years for mountains to grow. But many are shrinking every day. Mountains are being worn away by wind, frost, and ice. They attack the peaks and break off chips of rock.

Shrinking mountain

The life of a river

Flowing rivers
Rivers begin as fast-flowing streams high up on mountainsides. Some streams bubble up from below the ground. Others flow from lakes or trickle from the tips of melting glaciers. The start of a river is called its source.

Sandy deserts
Most deserts are not sandy but covered in gravel and stones. In some deserts there are high mountains or strange-shaped rocks rising from the ground.

Desert landscapes

The Amazon river

Islands
Indonesia in South East Asia is made up of more than 13,000 islands.

A coral island

A very long river
The Amazon river in South America is 3,977 miles long.

DESTRUCTIVE EARTH

People used to believe that floods, tidal waves, and earthquakes were sent by angry gods to punish them. By studying winds, tides, rocks, and weather, scientists have begun to understand the awesome forces behind natural disasters.

Pompeii, AD 79

Avalanche

Avalanche!
If snow gets too heavy, it can suddenly break loose, crash downhill, and slide. But other things can trigger an avalanche. A skier or even a car door being slammed can set the snow sliding. Avalanches can slide at speeds of up to 200 mph, as fast as a race car. Hundreds of tons of snow hurtle down the slope.

Layers of snow and ice build up then slip away

An Atlantic hurricane hits the island of Antigua
Hurricanes can be enormous. Some measure 1,800 miles wide and even the smallest are about half the width of Great Britain. Winds inside a hurricane can blow at over 187 mph. Hurricanes are named from an alphabetical list. A new list is made every year. The names of the worst hurricanes, like Andrew or Carol, are never used again.

Kobe earthquake, Japan, 1995

Earthquakes
Big earthquakes do lots of damage. Huge cracks open up in the ground. Houses, roads, and bridges shake and fall down. In the worst earthquakes, many people are killed and injured by buildings that collapse on top of them.

Death of Pompeii
In AD 79, Mt Vesuvius in Italy blew its top in a massive explosion. The nearby city of Pompeii was buried under a huge cloud of hot ash and rock. Thousands of people were suffocated. Others fled for their lives.

Fault lines
Fault runs through the Earth's crust.

Crust tries to move.

Stage 1

Pressure builds up.

Stage 2

Earthquake finally occurs as pieces move apart with a jerk.

Stage 3

Town covered in ash after eruption of Mt Pinatubo, Philippines

Dangerous neighbour
Despite the danger, many people all over the world live near volcanoes. The ash that erupts from a volcano makes the soil very rich–ideal for growing crops. A volcano that still erupts is called active. An extinct volcano is one that is never likely to erupt again.

Sleeping volcanoes
Some volcanoes sleep for hundreds or even thousands of years. A sleeping volcano is said to be dormant. But it can wake up at any minute.

Cross-section of a Volcano

Inside a volcano
Volcanoes are mountains that spit fire. Deep under the Earth there is red-hot, runny rock called magma. Sometimes the magma bursts up through a crack in the Earth's crust and a volcano erupts.

Mt St Helen's, USA was a dormant volcano that erupted

Landslides
A landslide is a huge fall of sliding soil or mud that suddenly breaks off a cliff or mountainside. Some landslides are caused by volcanoes, heavy rain, or earthquakes, which make the ground shake and move.

Earthquake warning
An earthquake sends shock waves rippling through the ground. Scientists study these waves to see how big the earthquake is. They measure earthquakes on a scale of 1 to 10. Each quake on the scale is 30 times worse than the one before.

Landslide

Cliff collapsing into the sea

Cracked Earth
The Earth's rocky crust is cracked into several gigantic pieces and lots of smaller chunks that drift on the red-hot molten rock below. The large pieces contain the seven continents–Africa, Antarctica, Asia, Australasia, Europe, North America, and South America.

Collapsing cliffs
As the waves crash against a cliff, they wear away the bottom of the cliff. If the cliff becomes too topheavy, it collapses into the sea. Along the east coast of England, cliff-top villages have toppled into the sea.

Seismograph (earthquake measuring device)

Earth's main continental plates

43

AMAZING WEATHER

The weather on our planet is amazing. Most of the time it is peaceful and calm. However, when rough weather strikes it can bring complete cities to a standstill and destroy whole areas of land.

Tsunamis
The Japanese word tsunami means "harbor wave" because of the way they crash into the harbor. They are also called tidal waves. Underwater earthquakes create fast waves that get higher close to the land. They can be 98 feet high and 124 miles long. Some race across the sea at about 560 mph.

Don't get carried away
When a tsunami hits land, watch out! It smashes down on to the shore, washing houses, people, and boats away.

Boat stranded inland

Speedy tornado
Most tornadoes travel at about 19 mph, but some move much faster. They race along the ground as quickly as a car. What's more, the wind inside a tornado can blow at an amazing 300 mph.

Leaving a trail of damage

Tsunami cutaway

Cliffs worn by waves

Wave power
As the wind and waves wash against the cliffs, they wear them down. Over a long period of time this action makes sand.

Hurricanes
Hurricanes are giant storms that begin over warm tropical seas. They are like huge, spinning wheels of wind, rain, and clouds. They sweep across the sea, then begin to die down when they reach land.

Cutaway of a hurricane

Eye of the hurricane
The eye of the hurricane is a patch of calm, clear weather in the hurricane's center. As the eye passes over land, there's a break in the storm for an hour or so. then it begins again.

Eye of hurricane seen from space

Sand power
Windblown sand dunes creep forward every year and can bury whole desert villages.

Sand dunes covering a town

Sandstorms
A sandstorm is a thick, choking cloud of sand whipped up by the wind in the desert.

Sandstorm in Africa

Lightning strike

Flash floods
Flash floods happen very suddenly, with no warning. Sometimes there isn't time to evacuate buildings in the flood's path. In 1955, a flood in the USA washed a four-story wooden hotel clean away.

Flash flood, Ouveze River, France

Thunder and lightning
Lightning is about five times hotter than the Sun's surface. As it streaks through the sky, it heats the air so quickly that it makes a loud booming sound. This is the sound of thunder.

Molten lava
Magma erupting from a volcano is called lava. It can be thick and lumpy or thin and runny. In the air, it cools and turns into hard, black rock.

Volcano erupting

Blizzards
A blizzard is a snowstorm. Strong winds blow the snow into drifts and it can be difficult to see. People and traffic can't move about, and schools and offices have to be closed.

Battling against a blizzard

Hailstorms
A hailstone is a small ball of ice that starts life in a thundercloud. Inside the cloud, a chip of ice is tossed up and down many times. It gets coated in layers of ice. The biggest hailstone was the size of a watermelon. It fell in Kansas, USA, in 1970.

Record-breaking hailstone

Build-up of hailstone in thundercloud

Geysers
Geysers are giant jets of scalding water and steam. They exist in places with lots of volcanoes. The red-hot rocks underground heat water far below the surface until it's so hot it shoots through a crack.

Geyser in Yellowstone Park, USA

OTHER PLANETS

People once thought Earth was at the center of the Universe. Now we know Earth is one of many planets moving through space. All the different planets have their own strong, natural forces just like Earth.

Side of Milky Way galaxy seen from deep space

Our galaxy
The Milky Way is a spiral galaxy. Viewed from above, it looks like a giant cake with swirls of white icing. From the side, it looks more like two fried eggs stuck back-to-back!

Jupiter and Earth

Jupiter
Jupiter is so big that all the other planets in the Solar System could fit inside it! It is made up of gases with a small, rocky core. The Great Red Spot is a storm larger than Earth. It has been raging for over 300 years!

Search for Extra-Terrestrial Intelligence (SETI)
Life might be such a fluke that it only exists on Earth. But if scientists can find just one other place where there is life, we'll know life's no accident–and that there could be millions of aliens!

Alien life?

Radio telescopes

Mercury
Mercury is about the same size as our Moon and is the planet closest to the sun. It zooms around the Sun in just 88 days, at an incredible 108,000 mph.

Mercury and Earth

Venus
Venus is a fraction smaller than Earth. A day on Venus lasts 243 Earth days, but a year is only 225 Earth days. Venus was named after the Roman goddess of love and beauty.

Venus and Earth

Radio astron...

Mars and...

Saturn and Earth

Seeing the Solar System
Humans can't travel to other planets yet. Instead, unmanned space probes send home pictures of the planets.

Voyager probe passing Neptune

Saturn
You could fit about 740 Earths into Saturn. It is the second largest planet. Its rings are 167,000 miles wide– about twice the width of the planet. Saturn is so light that it would float on water like a boat!

Cassini probe carrying the Huygens probe to Titan

Probing for life
The Huygens probe will parachute on to Saturn's largest moon, Titan, in 2004. Titan has a cloudy atmosphere and might be covered in an ocean.

Moon Base
As the Moon is only three days away and has low gravity it is easy to land spacecraft there. One day a Moon Base might be built so people could live there.

Is anyone there?
People all around the world spend their time on computers, studying waves from space, hoping to find alien messages.

Moon Base

Uranus
In 1781 William Herschel discovered Uranus. Because it is tilted on its side, the poles are the warmest places. Summer at the South Pole lasts 42 years!

Uranus and Earth

Neptune
At 2.8 billion miles away from the Sun, Neptune is bitterly cold. Very, very strong winds rip across the surface all the time, much faster than any winds on Earth.

Neptune

Exploring Mars
The Mars Pathfinder (1997) had a small, six-wheeled rover, called Sojourner. It used a camera and laser beams to find its way around on the surface.

Mars
Mars was named after the Roman god of war, because of its blood-red color. Though there are no seas on Mars, there may be frozen water underground.

Pluto
Pluto is so far away that it takes 248 years just to orbit the sun once! At 1,466 miles across, it is smaller than the United States or Russia!

Pluto and Earth

CREDITS & ACKNOWLEDGMENTS

This is a Parragon Publishing Book
First published in 2003

Parragon Publishing
Queen Street House
4 Queen Street
Bath BA1 1HE, UK

Copyright © Parragon 2003

This book was created by

David West Children's Books

This edition was designed and produced by
Joshua Smith (JSG.net)

All rights reserved. No part of this publication may be reproduced, stored in a retrieval system, or transmitted by any means, electronic, mechanical, photocopying, recording or otherwise, without the prior permission of the copyright holder.

British Library Cataloguing-in-Publication Data

A catalogue record for this book is available from the British Library.

ISBN 1-40540-206-7

Printed in Malaysia